A BODY IN SPICE

ROSELINE MGBODICHINMA

This is a work of fiction. All names, characters, places, and incidents are a product of the author's imagination. Any resemblance to real events or persons, living or dead, is entirely coincidental.

Published by Akashic Books

ISBN: 978-1-63614-247-0

Printed in China
First printing

EU Authorized Representative details:
Easy Access System Europe
Mustamäe tee 50, 10621 Tallinn, Estonia
gpsr.request@easproject.com

Akashic Books
Instagram, X, Facebook: AkashicBooks
info@akashicbooks.com
www.akashicbooks.com

African Poetry Book Fund
Brown University
10 Prospect Street
Box A
Providence, RI 02912

TABLE OF CONTENTS

PREFACE

by Tsitsi Jaji

A Body in Spice may be Roseline Mgbodichinma's first chapbook, but it is also the work of a seasoned writer. Unified thematically, this chapbook incorporates forms ranging from the familiar to the wondrously original to meditate on desire, lineage, spirituality, and the meaning of home. Mgbodichinma is a sure guide through subject matter both explicit and esoteric; to say she is a tasteful writer only hints at the gorgeous language she offers. Dig in, but with caution—you may find yourself devouring the entire collection in one sitting.

Taste is in fact one of the central metaphors of the chapbook, and its title, *A Body in Spice*, evokes both the frisson of spicy speech and the pleasure of intense flavors that lips, teeth, and tongue savor in the best cooking. What results is a broad testimony ranging from cruelty to devotion. Many of these poems hit us in the gut, others throb with erotic power, but you will also find here the cerebral, the ambivalent, the bleak. The depths of depression are not utterly barren, but rather a space of knowledge and vision, and poetry is a way to survive the aftermath. This is courageous and necessary writing.

The collection speaks to the many worlds within and beyond Africa. Mgbodichinma explores a global spectrum, with poems dedicated to writers on both sides of the Atlantic. The chapbook begins with a ghazal and ends with two poems answering, with bracing specificity, the questions "Why I Do Not Write Happy Poems" and "What Happiness Means to Me." In the latter, concluding poem, Mgbodichinma begins in the mouth, with "a seasoned pepper soup bowl that makes me snort." She goes on to declare that faith, family, and friends are as much sustenance as the "juicy protein in a plate of stew." Throughout the chapbook, we read that healing only begins in pain. The fundamental human need to be loved means that before we can be free, we must imagine freedom.

And what frees us is what brings happiness. Art has power: as Mgbodichinma writes, "never being body-shamed" makes photographing her own image and "being photographed by someone who loves me" a gesture of joyous liberation.

This is exactly what the eleven years of box sets in the *New-Generation African Poets* series have given us—many little bundles of joy. Writing this introduction as one of the poets in the inaugural box set, I am thrilled when Mgbodichinma's evocations of kitchen spaces, matrilineage, and sexual trauma recall the brilliant, shattering collections by Ladan Osman and Warsan Shire. The box sets turn each cluster of writers from multiple geographies into a new understanding of Africa as potential, relationship, exchange, and vision. A writer residing in Nigeria, Mgbodichinma is anchored on the continent; she balances diasporic voices as the African Poetry Book Fund has sought to do, using multiple strategies to enact our common Africanness. Each year, the previous generation meets new poetic kin on the pages of another box set, as well as through initiatives such as readings, the African Poetry Digital Portal, and poetry libraries on the continent. The sum of these efforts is feeding African poetry. Writing as a Zimbabwean-American woman in North Carolina, I am immensely proud to introduce you to my Nigerian sister, and to celebrate such delectable work with you lucky readers. Enjoy!

A GHAZAL IN YESES

The cost of living is a ruthless {yes}
Death proposes heaven to me, I accept—a clueless {yes}

In a nightmare, cinnamon tries to asphyxiate me & fails
I wake up with a nosebleed, Alive? I yell a breathless {yes}

Once, in a magical crowd, I saw a vision the depth of a root,
I spew out dreams, the universe lets out a careless {yes}

I prayed to be sensitive & my body became a mimosa
A man stroked my arms, I folded—an airless {yes}

{Y = mx + b} where m is my body, x is death, & b is god
Solving for y in this wild world is pointless {yes?}

I am salty when love holds me close in heat
It rains; a lover reaches—I moan a flawless {yes}

Lust is the color of a man-made lake
Pour into me & I you, let our bodies whisper a zipless {yes}

Dark matter, gray matter, no matter; my life unconscious
Please offer me sentience—I'll scream a helpless {yes}

Ocean love becomes a cup of brackish water & yet you ask:
Is love lost forever? The answer is an anchorless {yes}

Come humid, come dust, bad soul makes bad weather
There is more to salvation than a godless {yes}

Can two walk together unless they agree?
The answer is a mindless {yes}

My body, a case; I & a rose robin are dimorphic
Furnish me an immortal form—I'll bellow a deathless {yes}

DAMAGE IN CLOVES

I. Some women
use clove water
to purge their uterus of
old blood.

Not me, though;
my womb is retainer
& my stale blood
is ichor
There will be glory in
the third heavens
when my flow stops
attempting
murder.

II. Cloves are
nail-shaped
flower buds

Nail-shaped as metaphor
for the cross my body
becomes
when men decide
darkness
is the best time
to crucify
me,

Flower buds
the shape of my clitoris
atrophying at my lover's
touch.

III. The flower
buds mature in
hue over time
and become ripe
for collecting
when they turn
vibrant red.
Cloves are
handpicked
before **the** flower
opens.

Replace *Cloves* with *I*
are with *was*
the with *my*
& *open* with *opened*

- I was hand-
picked before
my flower
opened,

my woman body
is nature's wager
& the best man never wins

you see;
_____) hand-picked me
_____) hand-picked me
_____) hand-picked me

- Before my flower
opened, someone
hand-picked me.

Lord knows my trauma
is still in active voice.

GOSPEL ACCORDING TO SALT LAKE

Before, during, and after the Biafran War, Okposi supplied salt to all of Eastern Nigeria.

two hunters find body of water / two hunters stoop for drink / two hunters almost die from too much salt / two hunters run to village / man like them argue / man like them want all glory / man like them want to name lake after them / hunter men ask god to name the first man among them / they ask: who found a lake first? / god demands a daughter to answer / trade by barter—brine for a body / saline for a soul / one hunter man offers his daughter & yet lake remains a pond / & a lake / & a pond / but never his name /

a lake, like a daughter, does not dry / a lake was war / a lake seasoned a civil war / the truth is salt was once water in a lake / daughters cooked pots of water till they became salt / an old daughter said foreigner drove to a lake & fetched lake water / foreigner's wheels stiffened & steering froze / old daughter says lake belongs only to them / old daughter says lake water cannot be fetched by others / old daughter says lake water can cure kwashiorkor / old daughter says lake water will flatten fat stomach / old daughter says lake water will heal the world / lake water must do whatever old daughter wills it /

old daughter bends & treks long miles for lake water / old daughter lights firewood & fans flames till lake water boils without end / old daughter is tired & it is young daughter's time of the month every day / god says bleeding daughters are taboo / lake never dries / a world is waiting for lake water to become salt / hunter men don't know how to boil lake water to become salt / old daughter dies & young daughter keeps on bleeding / lake water disappears.

POLLINATION

Footprints graze the earth in silence,
solitary walks, a muted green—the hue of silence.

I am no different than a startled snail,
I crawl into my body in silence.

In my garden, weed and produce are one & the same
bell peppers & clovers grow roots in silence.

I am like a tree planted in the middle of the river—isolated,
currents move estuaries in silence.

Petrichor leaves no one the language to read the rainbows,
colors become blessings in silence.

Sundays are for white, bare feet kissing holy ground,
sin is always confessed in silence.

I bury seeds only to resurrect them into devouring—sometimes,
I build only to tear down in silence.

I cling to myself like a seedless grapefruit, no space for pollination,
a rose nurses her thorns in silence.

REPENTING

Body made flesh & dwelling among us, the sweet-smelling savor of a breathless sacrifice. There is a street where the righteous lick their fingers, sweet as sin. Shallot sounds like a name used to describe a sex worker. Mathematically speaking, shallots are cross-dressers who are often ≠ onions + garlic. This flirtation is garnish. There is a joint in the east with layers that men go to cry. Perhaps this writing is an exotic dance. Garlic belongs everywhere except morning breath. A young girl hates poetry because the language is too flowery, but she accepts the scribblings of a lover. A dried flower is also a spice & is this wilting not also a poem? This poem may be about everything you {___} about godliness, a body is fundamentally flesh. Sometimes heaven is not a dwelling place, it is only an aroma, like shallot / like onions / like garlic. Let's end all prayers here.

A BLOODY PENCHANT

To damn my body
& conquer this world,
to make my waist into fennel
& pretend the current flowing
between my legs is not a
madhouse—I go to church.
There is prophecy
about painless periods.
Undoing is this red song
billowing between what is divine
& what may be an overflow.

Since the Holy Book says
God has a penchant for women
in blood & pain
I move to the altar,
I go to make my case,
I kneel & I say,
God, the Brahmaputra river
in India
turns blood-red for three days
in June every year,
gracious God,
why give a woman's rest
to a river?

But when a woman's body is an emmenagogue,
petition is merely a blood clot.
My uterus is a bounty hunter,

and every month I must pay for not bringing
a newborn into this world.
My lining breaks down in protest.
I bleed
& bleed
& bleed.

SAUCE PERSEVERING

". . . I am clanging, full
of kinks,
teeming with my own spice: turmeric, clove, paprika—
grains of paradise . . ."
—Tiana Clark

In this body, there is also joy. A mirror cracks at my reflection & my beauty grows in parts. On some mornings I am beautiful in bits. My broken face is a listing for light. My crooked smile is sunshine persevering.

In this body, there is also joy. My love handles hold water after each bath. When there is a famine my rolls may save me from drought.

In this body, there is also joy. My sauce has a mellow sweetness. When I sting, I sting in color. A woman tried to love me once; it came with a flavor I did not understand. I fled.

In this body, there is also joy. Orange is a happy color / I wear black instead. My neighbor, caramel-skinned / tints her moisturizer with turmeric / she just wants to be yellow.

In this body, there is also joy. I prefer my body unclad & clothed in feels. Like a touch without a tearing / a peel with no protrusion / caresses without inter-course / my frame is a starving woman yearning.

In this body, there is also joy. Because—a mirror cracks at my reflection / my love handles hold water after each bath / my sauce has a mellow sweetness /
orange is a happy
color & / I prefer my body unclad & clothed in feels.

LORD OF SALT

With reparation leaking from my lips
& knees the shape of amends,
                    God, I have no salinity
left in these bones this minute,
I lost my flavor to hungry men thirsting.
                    Please reconsider my crushing.
My seduction was merely a means—
to season the earth,
I must begin from a man's bosom.
God, I have not rebelled more than the man
who lost a hip wrestling for blessings.

So use me still,
use me tasteless.
Let me cause ruckus in earthly
places. Use this saltless
body for temptation.
It is tasteless after all.
Christen this body
a burning city
that men may behold it &
become pillars
of salt.

OSE-OJI

A boil grows the size of an Adam's apple
  & sits on my throat

My neck stiffens like a pipe
  & my voice is muted
My mother asks:
"Can you swallow salt water?"
"Does it hurt?"
"How much can you spit?"
"Is your voice still alive?"
I cannot answer
My mother calls her
mother,

Her mother says the solution
Is a visitation—is a removal
is ose-oji—is ogogoro—is her aged finger
  Drilling down my youthful
throat.
My mother's mother arrives. She lifts
my face,
Parts my mouth open, & forces
Pepper, alcohol, & water
Down my throat
{Here is a blur _____}
My sharp fingers dig into her
wrinkled skin
pus-filled screams escape
my throat,
My pupils dilate
My mother asks again
  "Does it hurt?"
I do not stop screaming!

A BRACKISH SILENCE

In your poetry workshop,
    the teacher unmutes himself and throws a word.
    He says—estuary: write a poem with estuary.
    You google this coastal body of water,
    how this tidal mouth of a river is your nemesis
    & prayer is a place where freshwater becomes saltwater.
    You try to understand the translations on your body.
    The burrowing on your chin is how you hold an amen to light,
    knowing your supplications will remain unanswered.
    Hallelujah is a brackish stream of consciousness,
    or how else does a mother raise her hands to God
while offering her child an elbow?
Silence is vernacular for loss
because you asked your mother how many times
you left her body before you became whole
and she said nothing.
Instead, she unearths herself
& points to a river as pale as your skin.
You stare at the conflation of water.
You wonder what parts of you were made from algae.

WHEN MY GRANDMOTHER BECOMES A GARDEN

Days are numbered in the crackling of bones.
Music flows through marrow
and rhythm becomes stifled heartbeats
when a person's breath starts to smell like
garlic, raw eggs, and wool.
It means the earth requires a dirge
and new roots must form from a farewell song.
The gray on my grandmother's head
sprouts like lilies.
Her teeth are no more than fallen blocks
when her spirit becomes a garden.
I want her to water down the thorns in my life,
and say to all the roses inside me,
your only job is to produce heart.

OGIRI OKPEI

Decay is also delicacy,
seasoned hands unwrap rot
from stale banana leaves in a mother's kitchen
        & a body flinches from offense.

A mouth-watering rudiment is
a stench,
meaning a lover tells another lover
sex is sweeter without two days' bath
& that *lover* agrees.

A lover thinks lovemaking is
cooking a local dish,
like ogiri okpei,
less pungent in the heat of passion.

In a mattress,
a lover's body thrusts
another lover's body flinches from disgust.

SPICE

May we be tasty, may we be soft.

Many magic days make our kind of decade.

For this mace love, I knelt & prayed.

Your deep luster touch came at no cost.

In your body, the depth of my eyes is lost.

I call you beautiful & your smile gets me laid.

King & Queen we do not checkmate.

Our soul ministers, our bodies are organ loft.

My womanhood, sweet like cinnamon

has frequent use for you.

Gloomy mornings expect your vengeful stroke.

In a wet dream, my hair is strung in a bun

& my thirsty essence has no clue

if your tasteful hands will this neck choke.

I JUST WANT YOU TO REMEMBER

Vanilla essence / Moringa tea / fudge-filled chocolate cake / then the naira
notes we stole from a salver / & didn't disappear like childhood superstitions.

You & me in that eatery holding our breath / like demigods paying for hunger
with the wind. We ordered soy milk with straws. Then a lighter for the smoke
about to glide through our paper cigarettes.

You were facing the pane, quiet / I am multilingual / yet I couldn't make sense
of your silences.

There is a bout between coming and becoming / so I don't have many ways to
tell you / that it was not the time my legs curved into a parachute

to welcome your candle / or the time you spelled your name on my cervix

with your fingers. Your smoking was how I knew / your tongue work could lead
me home / I fell first from your sip,

your saliva shyly curling over that straw / drops of soy on your beard.

In this moment / I just want you to remember the shimmer on that straw

as your mouth took long & slow sips.

So when we do our spicy flip / you'll please remind my body

how you took your last sip.

MISSING BODY REPORT

After "The Kitchen" by Warsan Shire

Bay leaves & broth steaming;
  just yesterday my body went missing.

Heated oil, onions sizzling;
  I saw it last on a bush path.

Curry paste & rosemary;
  the butcher said he knew where I left my retina.

Yaji & all-purpose;
  I don't want my eyesight, please give me my legs.

Thyme & coconut milk;
  he keeps chopping a bloodied limb.

Saffron & garlic;
  turn left, turn right, he points me down a dusty street.

Locust beans & uziza;
  there is no body there.

Cloves & palm oil bleaching;
  the butcher says he can trace my septum.

Cayenne & black pepper;
  fuck perception, please show me my hands.

Scent leave & lemongrass oozing;
  he points me to a local farm.

Scent leave & lemongrass oozing;
the butcher is freezing ten fingers.

I AM WANTED EVERYWHERE

After "Post Massacre Psyche Evaluation" by Abu Bakr Sadiq

Nobody asked me what it took them to slice me open.
There is a scarf I hold on to
when the crucifixion starts.
I let blood & water mix like wine
and when they ask me who tried to kill me,
or where the weapons are,
I will show them your tongue,
tell them your closed mouth is the sheath
and your smile, another kind of crimson.

Or don't you remember?
The mockery on that November morning,
how my tight dress became a circus
as you danced around me in blasphemies
saying there is no room for a belly as big as mine in a dress
as colorful as that.
Sometimes shaming is as potent as a bullet
& one shot is all it takes.

Do you know death has a fashion sense?
It is a garment of morphed wishes,
the one that wears itself on me when my lover says
we cannot make love with candles
because my body is not shaped like an hourglass.

Not all kinds of death lock you in a grave, some kinds
leave you roaming in the world?
I don't know what it means to have a deathless body

because every day, a part of me dies intestate.
My mother is afraid another man will shoot me
for living in this body. I, too, am afraid to exist
so I launch a police report.

I am writing my statement & the policeman says
I should show him evidence of attempted murder.
I start to undress
& show him my love handles.
I tell him this is where the conspiracy began.
I tell him my extra skin is their ammunition
& my cellulite, their shotgun.
But he does not believe.

I tell him to file a restraining order against the world
because I do not know to which extent this body will grow.
But he does not understand.
So I dress
and I say,
Look! Look! Look!
It all started from the size of my stomach,
now I am wanted everywhere.

AN ODE TO YAJI

Yaji tastes like the family reunion at which
you start to like your African aunties.
Crushed Bouillon Cubes + Garlic Powder
+ Smoked Paprika + White Pepper + Roasted Groundnut
+ Onion Powder + Ground Ginger + Hot Red Pepper
+ Kulikuli + Negro Pepper = *unexpected unity.*

Yaji is memory;
fried chicken in boarding school jollof,
a newspaper full of suya,
red & brown omelets—grilled fish,
seasoned veggies, & sometimes tea.

Yaji is your favorite auntie packing spice
into a container from her north to visit your east.
Yaji is the joy of arrival,
it is snatching the container from her
hands at the door & testing your guts.
One kilishi + one tablespoon of Yaji = *a fire in your bowels.*

Yaji is trigger warning,
it is waiting for your aunt to visit again.
Yaji is waiting.
Yaji is waiting in vain.
Yaji is the pain of ordering Yaji
from an Instagram vendor.
Yaji is Instagram Yaji not tasting like your auntie's Yaji.
Yaji is wanting to ask your auntie
why she chose dying in the north

over bringing you
Yaji!

EVERYWHERE

To my dearest Aunt Onyemaechi

Your absence aches more than skin tearing
just yesterday, in a dream, we unwrapped bouillon cubes.
Your nail polish still reminds me of tomatoes.
I want to write prayers like you, but did supplication save your life?
If you were anything like God, I would hunt for myrrh & aloes,
embalm your body in spice
& wait for you to rise on any third day.
It's four years going on forever
& in this poem, you do not exist with breath in your lungs.
In another poem your whiff will be absent.
Remembering you is a crosswise movement
& my grief, a pit-long devotion.
If memory were a thread,
I would weave every
recollection of your life
into a living, breathing
thing.

A CHECKLIST QUENCHING

"Soften your heart.
You need to be tender enough to soak up the flavors, temper enough to
mop up the juice.
You needn't be hard to swallow"
—Wana Udobang

Some dreams are tastier than others.
You say this to me over breakfast
as if to say everything I dream of is bland
& your fantasy is the best vision
for us.

You say the omelet lacks cheese
& you prefer a sunny-side up with sprinkles
of black pepper.
You would also prefer me in a tighter dress
& maybe a weave, more matte than gloss.

You like "girls" women
who walk two steps behind,
"girls" women
who never touch themselves,
"girls" women
who prop their legs in position
& let you be clueless
until coming,
"girls" women who fix you a plate
without wanting

to eat or needing you
to eat them,
"girls" women who become things
on your checklist.
Say:

    this baby must not stretch you beyond
    be bright as curry when my friends show
    cook up a storm & impress my mother
    call your sister-in-law auntie

You like "girls"
who are easy to swallow.

A FRIEND ASKS ME WHY I DO NOT WRITE HAPPY POEMS

- I once held faith in a plate of mustard seeds & no mountain moved.
- The seeds became a burning sensation & set my hope ablaze.
- Black mustard seeds are the spiciest in the mustard family, taking large amounts can damage the throat; yellow mustard seeds are preferred.
- I am already a large amount. I am black & not yellow, black & not yellow.
- The moon is my alibi for when laughter accuses me of hiding. It is not my fault joy only comes in the morning.
- Happiness is a river language & my throat is parched. My poetry flows through my belly & flow is a kind of faith & faith is the potential of many mustard seeds & too many mustard seeds inflame the guts.
- I am sore and sick for happiness.

THE SAME FRIEND ASKS ME WHAT HAPPINESS MEANS TO ME

It is a seasoned pepper soup bowl that makes me snort. It is juicy protein in a plate of stew. It is vanilla gelato in a heat wave. It is the crisp in a bag of salted chips. It is the feel of ice water gliding down my throat after a sunny day. It is peppery stew after a Sunday sermon. It is a hug from a sister. It is a long video chat with friends. It is the sanity of a brother. It is eating bread fresh from the oven. It is applying lip gloss on my juicy lips. It is the warmth of my mother's embrace. It is mind-mapping a father's love. It is never being body-shamed. It is photographing my body in a mirror. It is being photographed by someone who loves me. It is laughing at my own jokes. It is writing this poem. It is holding an answered prayer. It is listening to hymns & poetry. It is dancing alone in a room. It is watching people dance. It is buying a journal. It is watching black love on-screen. It is reading a good book. It is having a cool nap. It is reading a handwritten letter. Happiness is all this but never everything.

ACKNOWLEDGMENTS

Early versions of "Pollination," "A Bloody Penchant," "A Brackish Silence," and "I Am Wanted Everywhere" have appeared in the *Hellebore*, *Isele Magazine*, the *Willowherb Review*, and *SWWIM* respectively.